How to Sparkle at
ADDITION & SUBTRACTION TO 20

Moira Wilson

We hope you and your class enjoy using this book. Other books in the series include:

Maths titles

How to Sparkle at Beginning Multiplication and Division	978 1 897675 30 4
How to Sparkle at Counting to 10	978 1 897675 27 4
How to Sparkle at Maths Fun	978 1 897675 86 1
How to Sparkle at Number Bonds	978 1 897675 34 2

Science titles

How to Sparkle at Assessing Science	978 1 897675 20 5
How to Sparkle at Science Investigations	978 1 897675 36 6

English titles

How to Sparkle at Alphabet Skills	978 1 897675 17 5
How to Sparkle at Grammar and Punctuation	978 1 897675 19 9
How to Sparkle at Nursery Rhymes	978 1 897675 16 8
How to Sparkle at Phonics	978 1 897675 14 4
How to Sparkle at Prediction Skills	978 1 897675 15 1
How to Sparkle at Reading Comprehension	978 1 897675 44 3
How to Sparkle at Word Level Activities	978 1 897675 90 8
How to Sparkle at Writing Stories and Poems	978 1 897675 18 2

Festive title

How to Sparkle at Christmas Time	978 1 897675 62 5

Published by Brilliant Publications
Unit 10, Sparrow Hall Farm, Edlesborough, Dunstable, Bedfordshire LU6 2ES

Sales and stock enquiries	Tel:	01202 712910
	Fax:	0845 1309300
Sales and payments	Email:	brilliant@bebc.co.uk
	Website:	www.brilliantpublications.co.uk
General enquiries:	Tel:	01525 222292

The name Brilliant Publications and its logo are registered trade marks.

Written by Moira Wilson
Illustrated by Moira Wilson

Printed in the UK

© Moira Wilson 1998
ISBN 978 1 897675 28 1

First published in 1998
Reprinted 2000, 2007
10   9   8   7   6   5   4   3

Contents

Introduction

This book contains a rich variety of activity sheets and games which will enable children to become competent at adding and subtracting to 20. Addition and subtraction are dealt with together because they are inextricably linked, one being the reverse operation of the other. Each section of the book, clearly labelled in the contents list, deals with a different aspect of addition and subtraction.

Early addition and subtraction to 10 Pages 6 to 12 introduce addition and subtraction in pictorial form. Various models are used: finding more and less; adding members of subsets; and counting on/back.

Investigating number bonds to 10 Pages 13 to 20 require the children to investigate number combinations for numbers 3 to 10 by way of: adding more objects pictorially to make a given number; arranging a group of objects in different ways; and finding all possible number combinations for a given whole number.

Reinforcement to 10 Pages 21 to 26 provide essential reinforcement. In order to complete the tasks, the children need to use and develop their knowledge of number facts to 10.

Investigating number bonds to 20 Pages 27 to 32 offer greater challenge by sometimes requiring the children to find three or four numbers bonded together to make given whole numbers or by restricting the numbers that they are allowed to use. Pages 33 to 36 require the children to solve 'missing number' problems using either addition or subtraction.

Reinforcement to 20 Pages 37 to 44 provide opportunities for the children to practise and develop their addition and subtraction skills to 20.

Games Pages 45 to 48, by introducing an element of chance, allow the children to consolidate the skills which they have learned in a fun, stimulating way.

Links to the National Curriculum

Close reference has been made to the National Curriculum in the writing of this book. The activities relate to the following programmes of study for Key Stage 1:

Pupils should be given opportunities to:

Using and applying mathematics
2a   select and use the appropriate mathematics;
2b   select and use mathematical equipment and materials;
3b   relate numerals and other mathematical symbols, eg '+' and '−' to a range of situations;
3d   use a variety of forms of mathematical presentation.

Number
3c   know addition and subtraction facts to 20;
3d   develop a variety of methods for adding and subtracting;
4a   understand the operations of addition, subtraction as taking away and comparison, and the relationship between them, recognize situations to which they apply and use them to solve problems with whole numbers.

Successful linking of the activities to the programmes of study depends to some extent on the way they are presented to children and subsequent adult input. The page entitled 'How to use this book' explores this in further detail.

How to use this book

The activities in this book are designed to supplement and enrich any core mathematics scheme. There is built-in progression but it is not essential that a child should complete every page or that the pages should be used in a certain order. Rather, the book is intended to be a 'dip-in' resource which you can use to give children support, practice or consolidation as and when you feel it is necessary.

The worksheets can be used with individuals or groups and you should first discuss the instructions with the children and show them examples of the task they are required to do. When involved in the task, the children should be encouraged to use specific language associated with addition and subtraction such as 'add', 'take away', 'equals', 'difference', 'count on/back', 'altogether' and 'more/less'.

It cannot be stressed too much that the activity sheets should always be preceded by practical work using real objects. The children will then have experiences upon which to draw when concepts are later treated in a more abstract way. Some children will benefit from using real objects when they are actually in the process of completing the sheets.

Although the pages are mostly self-explanatory, the following notes about certain activities may prove useful.

Pages 33 and 34
The children can be encouraged to use both addition and subtraction to solve the missing number problems by:
* counting on to the 'whole' number;
* counting back from the 'whole' number.
The task will be simplified by using real objects or number lines.

Pages 35 and 36
The idea of a 'missing number' is taken a step further. The pyramids and hats can only be successfully completed if a logical order is followed. Some children will need a good deal of preliminary discussion before attempting these activities.

Pages 37 and 38
Some children may notice a pattern emerging as they complete the squares but others may need help. They should be encouraged to look at:
* totals of diagonal numbers;
* totals of rows;
* totals of columns;
* bottom left and top right digits (addition squares);
* bottom right and top left digits (subtraction squares).

When completed and dated, the pages can be stored in the children's mathematics folders, creating a useful record of work covered.

More and more

Draw 2 more objects in each box and write the total number.

	total

Happy and sad

Count the objects and write the numbers in the boxes.

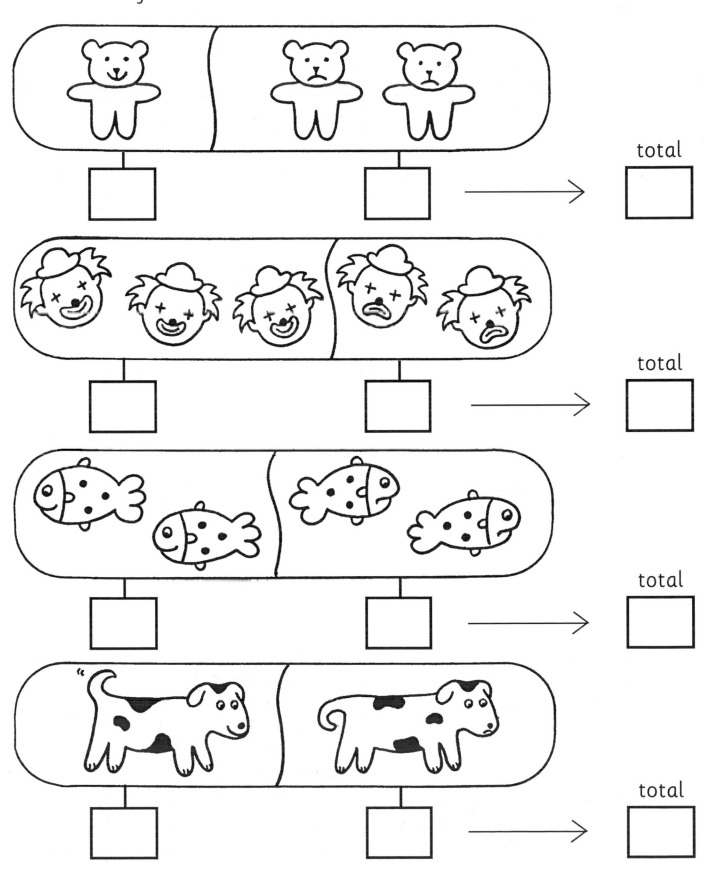

total

total

total

total

Spotty dominoes

Count the spots on each domino and write the numbers in the boxes.

⬚ 2 + 5 = 7	⬚ ☐ + ☐ = ☐
⬚ ☐ + ☐ = ☐	⬚ ☐ + ☐ = ☐
⬚ ☐ + ☐ = ☐	⬚ ☐ + ☐ = ☐
⬚ ☐ + ☐ = ☐	⬚ ☐ + ☐ = ☐

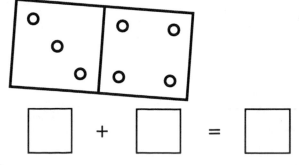

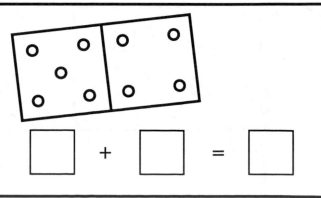

Kangaroo jumps

Help the kangaroo to jump to the correct stones.

Start on 3. Jump **forward** 4 stones. → ☐

1 2 3 4 5 6 7 8 9 10

Start on 6. Jump forward 3 stones. → ☐

1 2 3 4 5 6 7 8 9 10

Start on 2. Jump forward 4 stones. → ☐

1 2 3 4 5 6 7 8 9 10

Start on 1. Jump forward 7 stones. → ☐

1 2 3 4 5 6 7 8 9 10

Start on 5. Jump forward 3 stones. → ☐

1 2 3 4 5 6 7 8 9 10

Start on 4. Jump forward 6 stones. → ☐

1 2 3 4 5 6 7 8 9 10

Less and less

Cross out 2 objects in each box and write the number of objects left.

	objects left
(4 socks)	
(7 airplanes)	
(3 dogs)	
(6 worms)	
(5 ducks)	

Bunny jumps

Help the rabbits to jump to the correct stones.

Start on 9. Jump **back** 3 stones. → ☐

(1) (2) (3) (4) (5) (6) (7) (8) (9) (10)

Start on 7. Jump back 4 stones. → ☐

(1) (2) (3) (4) (5) (6) (7) (8) (9) (10)

Start on 4. Jump back 2 stones. → ☐

(1) (2) (3) (4) (5) (6) (7) (8) (9) (10)

Start on 10. Jump back 5 stones. → ☐

(1) (2) (3) (4) (5) (6) (7) (8) (9) (10)

Start on 6. Jump back 2 stones. → ☐

(1) (2) (3) (4) (5) (6) (7) (8) (9) (10)

Start on 8. Jump back 7 stones. → ☐

(1) (2) (3) (4) (5) (6) (7) (8) (9) (10)

Bags of fruit

Cross out the fruit that you eat and write the number left.

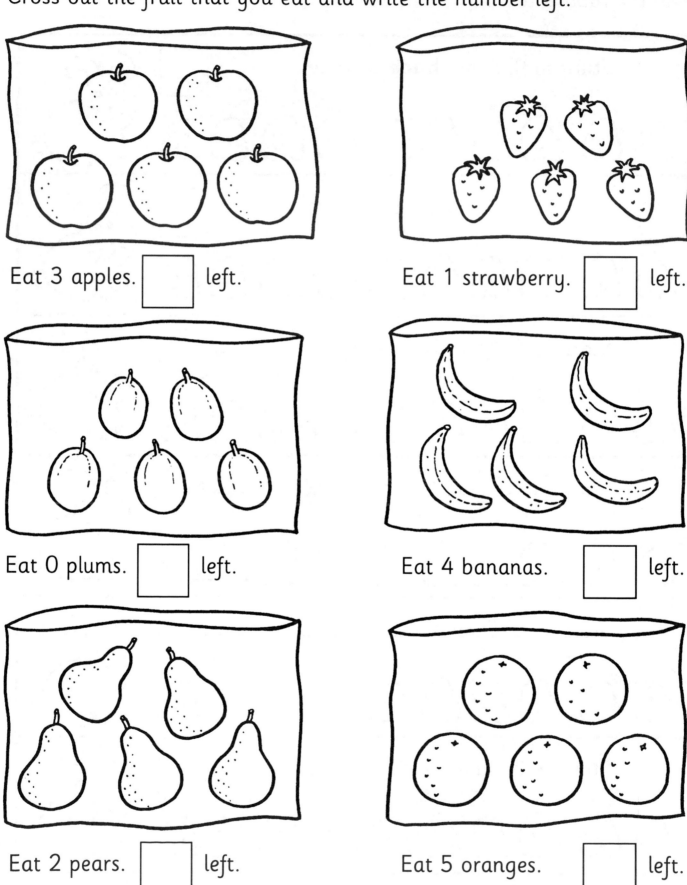

Eat 3 apples. ☐ left.

Eat 1 strawberry. ☐ left.

Eat 0 plums. ☐ left.

Eat 4 bananas. ☐ left.

Eat 2 pears. ☐ left.

Eat 5 oranges. ☐ left.

Gardening time

Make each tub have 3 flowers.

Make each twig have 3 leaves.

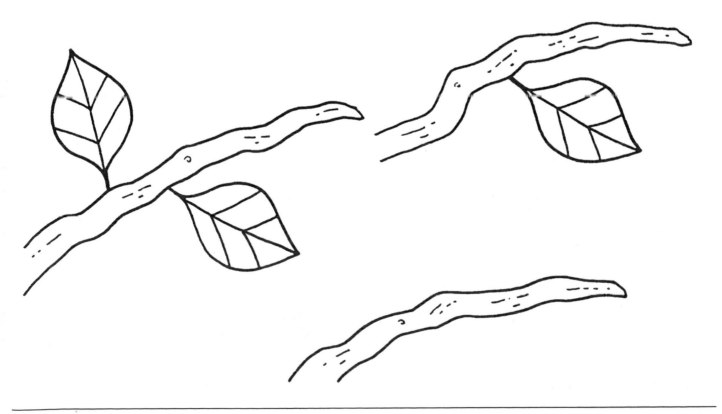

Party time

Make each party hat have 4 spots.
Make each cracker have 4 wavy lines.

Birthday time

Make each cake have 5 candles.
Write the number of candles you added.

3 and ☐

0 and ☐

2 and ☐

4 and ☐

5 and ☐

1 and ☐

Mini-beast hunt

Draw rings round the mini-beasts to show ways of making 6.
Make each one different.

□   and   □   make   □

□   and   □   make   □

□   and   □   make   □

□   and   □   make   □

□   and   □   make   □

Clumsy clowns

Find two numbers that add up to 7.
Make each sum different.

Colour the clowns hats blue if you have 0 in the sum
yellow if you have 1 in the sum
red if you have 2 in the sum
green if you have 3 in the sum.

Windy days

Find two numbers that add up to 8.
Make each sum different.

___ + ___ = 8

___ + ___ = 8

___ + ___ = 8

___ + ___ = 8

___ + ___ = 8

___ + ___ = 8

___ + ___ = 8

___ + ___ = 8

___ + ___ = 8

Crunchy apples

Find two numbers that add up to 9.
Make each sum different.

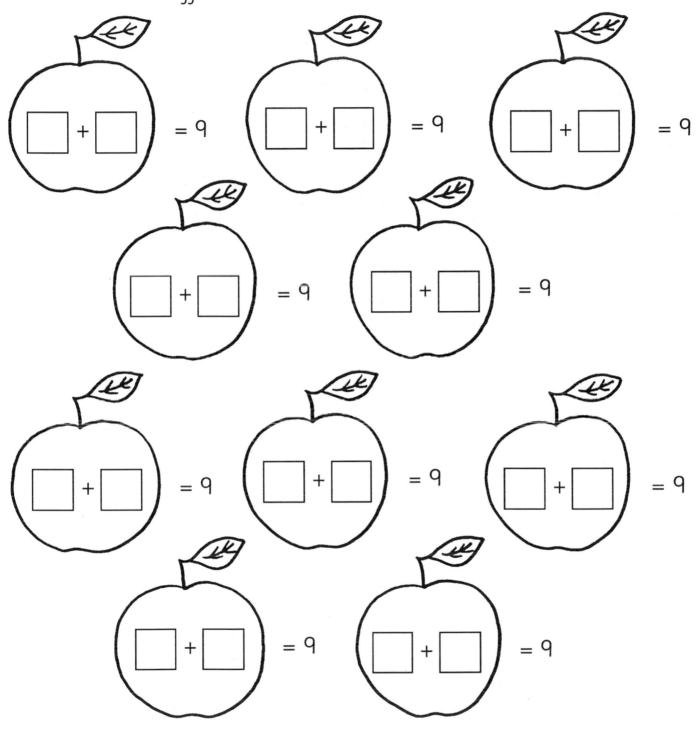

Colour the apples red if you have 0, 1 or 2 in the sum
green if you have 3 or 4 in the sum.

Rugged rocks

Find two numbers that add up to 10.
Make each sum different.

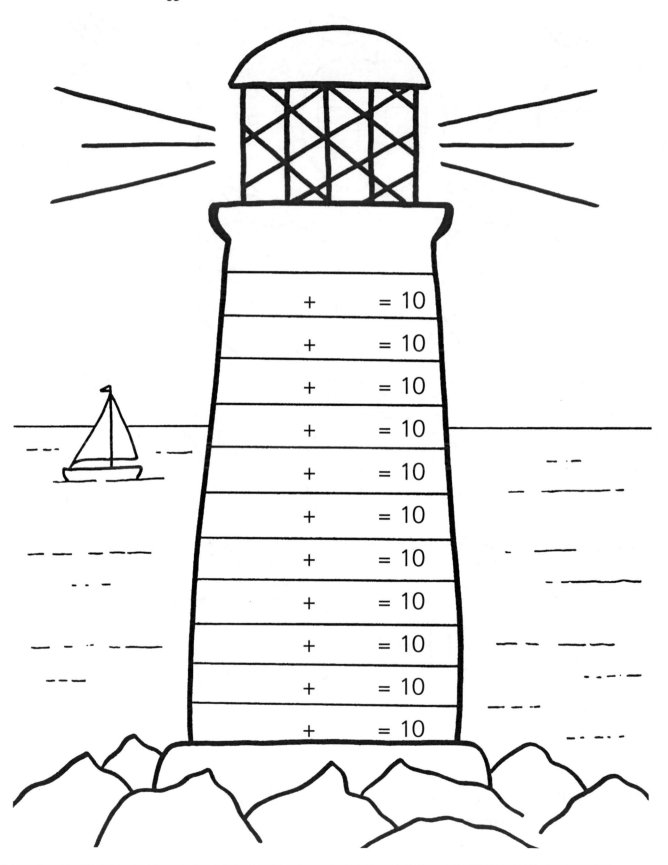

On the lighthouse, eleven rows each read:

+ ___ = 10

Flowers

Colour the leaves if the numbers on them add up to the number on the flower.

More flowers

Colour the petals if the difference is the same as the number in the middle.

Spotty dog

5 + 4

2 + 5

1 + 7

4 + 6

4 + 4

8 + 1

5 + 2

5 + 5

1 + 6

3 + 6

8 + 2

1 + 9

6 + 2

5 + 3

3 + 4

2 + 7

Colour the shapes green if the total is 7
blue if the total is 8
orange if the total is 9
brown if the total is 10.

Beautiful butterfly

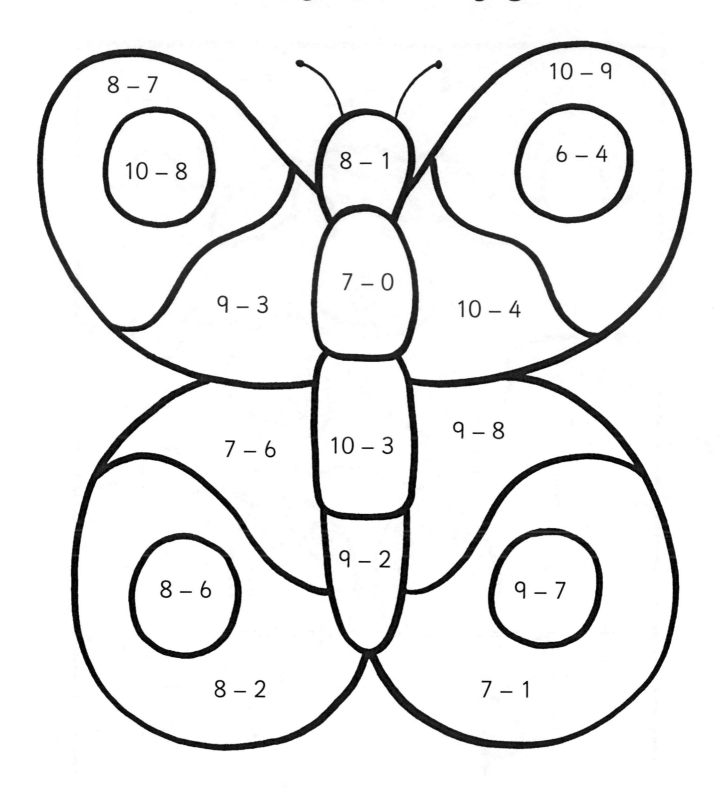

Colour the shapes yellow if the difference is 1
red if the difference is 2
green if the difference is 6
black if the difference is 7.

Which way is it?

Add up the numbers in each road. Colour the road where the total is the same as the number on the car.

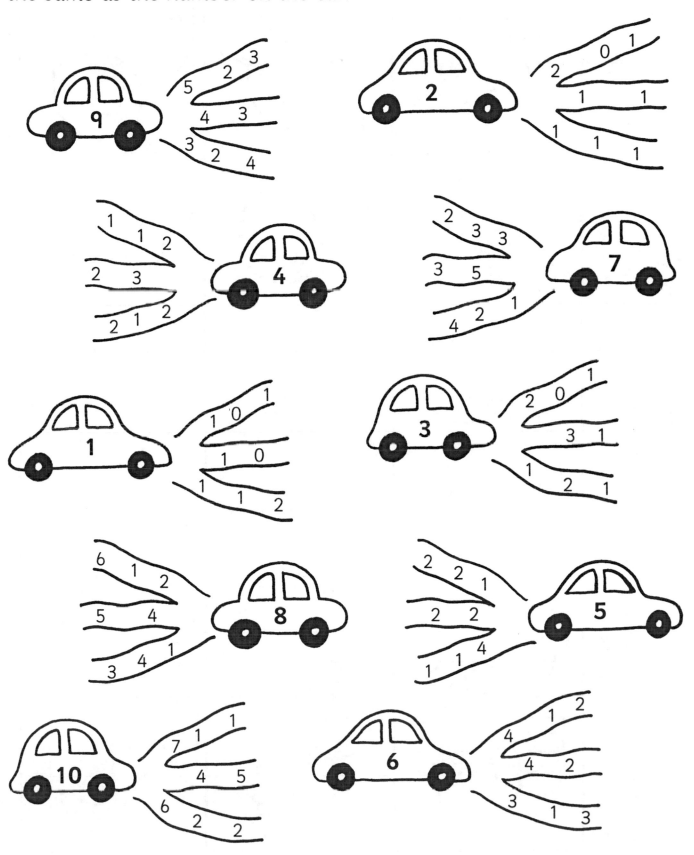

Mini-beast walk

Starting with the number on each mini-beast, take it for a walk, adding and subtracting as you go. Write the numbers in the leaves.

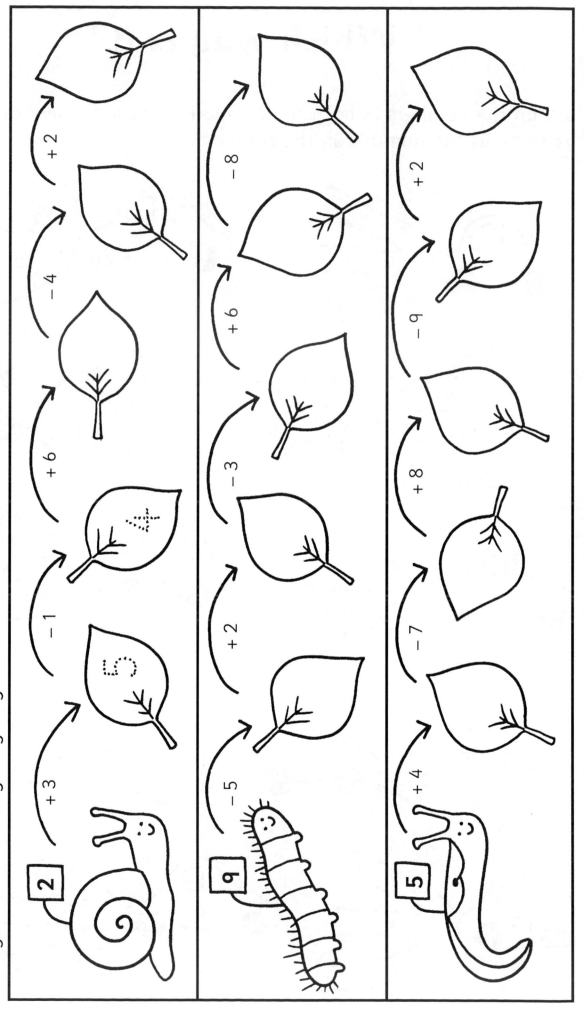

Bicycle wheels

Find two numbers that make the number in the middle.
Write them between the spokes.

Spiders' webs

Find three numbers that make the number in the middle.
Write them in the web.

Busy butterflies

The numbers on each butterfly should add up to $\boxed{15}$.
Make each butterfly different.

At the station

Make the number on each engine using addition and subtraction.

19   7 + 12   −   +   −

+   −   +   −   12

15   +   −   +   −

+   −   +   −   13

18   +   −   +   −

Candles

Make all the numbers to 20 choosing from the numbers
1, 2, 3 and 4 and the symbols + and −.
You can use each number and symbol more than once.

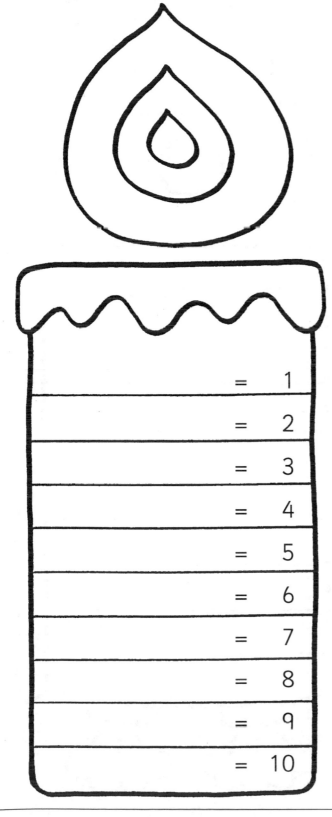

	=	1
	=	2
	=	3
	=	4
	=	5
	=	6
	=	7
	=	8
	=	9
	=	10

4 + 4 + 4 − 1	=	11
	=	12
	=	13
	=	14
	=	15
	=	16
	=	17
	=	18
	=	19
	=	20

Rockets

Make all the numbers to 20 choosing from the numbers
2 and 3 and the symbols + and −.
You can use each number and symbol more than once.

= 1	3 + 3 + 3 + 3 + 3 − 2 − 2 = 11
= 2	= 12
= 3	= 13
= 4	= 14
= 5	= 15
= 6	= 16
= 7	= 17
= 8	= 18
= 9	= 19
= 10	= 20

Ice-cream cones

Make the numbers on the ice-cream scoops add up to the number on the cone.

Kites

Make the numbers on each kite add up to the number in the middle.

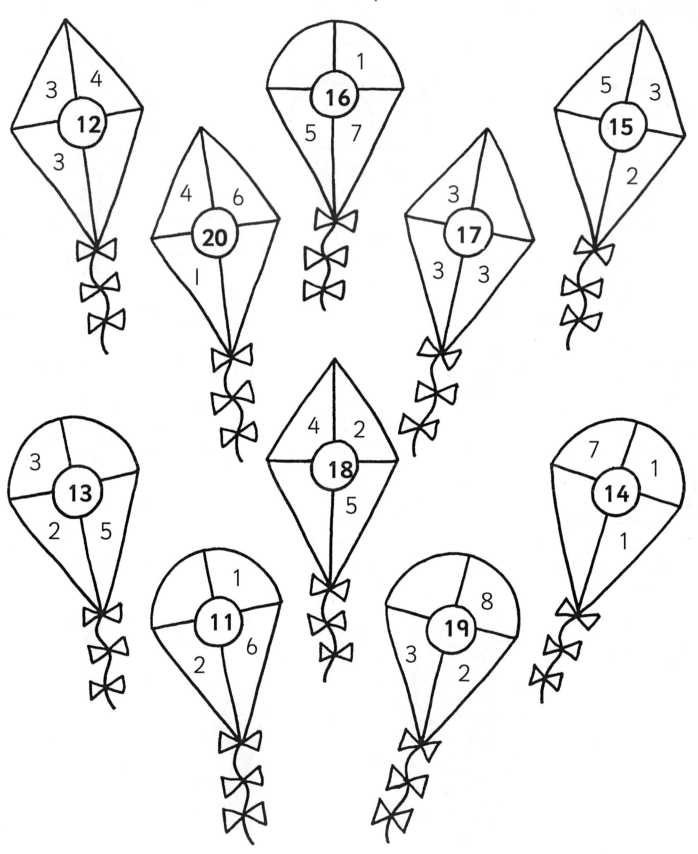

Pyramids

Write numbers in the empty building blocks. Make the number in each building block the total of the two numbers below it.

Magic hats

Make the numbers in each row, column and diagonal add up to the number on the star.

Addition squares

Add the numbers at the top to those at the side.

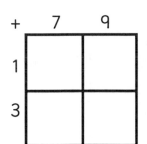

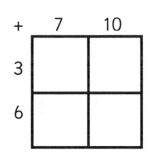

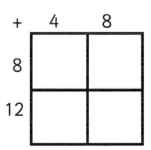

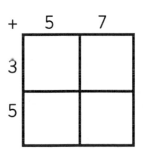

<table>
</table>

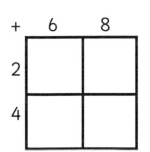

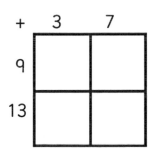

<table>
</table>

Look at the numbers in the squares. Can you see a pattern?

Subtraction squares

Take the numbers at the top away from those at the side.

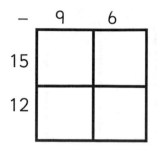

$-$ 9 6
15
12

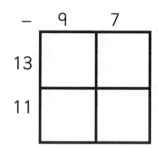

$-$ 9 7
13
11

$-$ 6 2
14
10

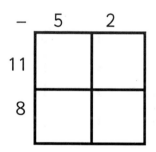

$-$ 5 2
11
8

$-$ 10 8
14
12

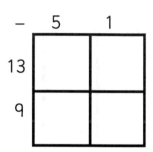

$-$ 5 1
13
9

$-$ 6 3
12
9

$-$ 8 6
12
10

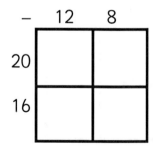

$-$ 12 8
20
16

Look at the numbers in the squares.
Can you see a pattern?

Where is my home?

Add up the numbers in each burrow. Colour the burrow where the total is the same as the number on the rabbit.

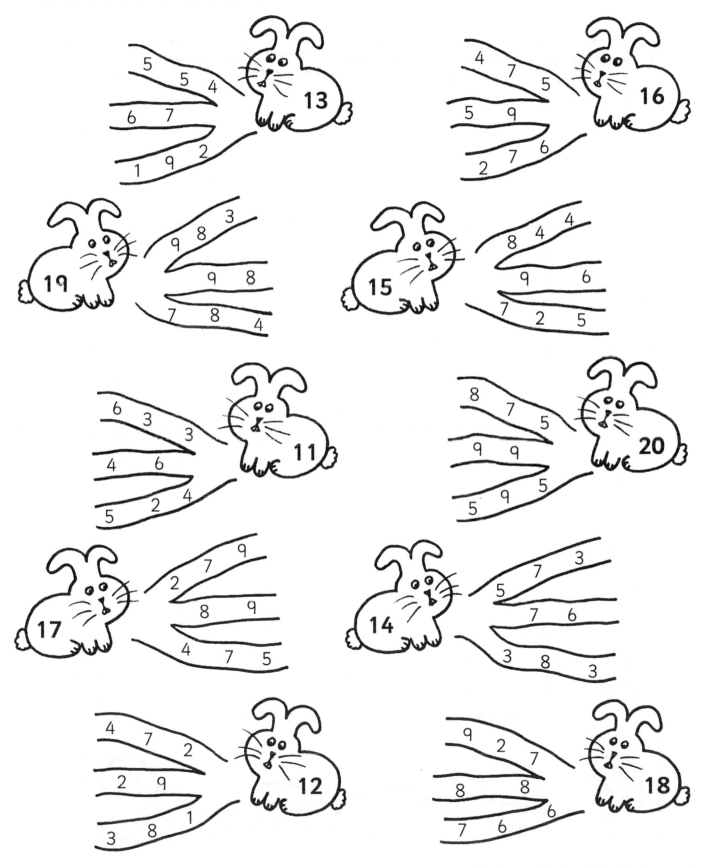

Mystery mosaic

If the difference between the two numbers in each square is 3, 4 or 5, colour the square. You will then discover the mystery picture.

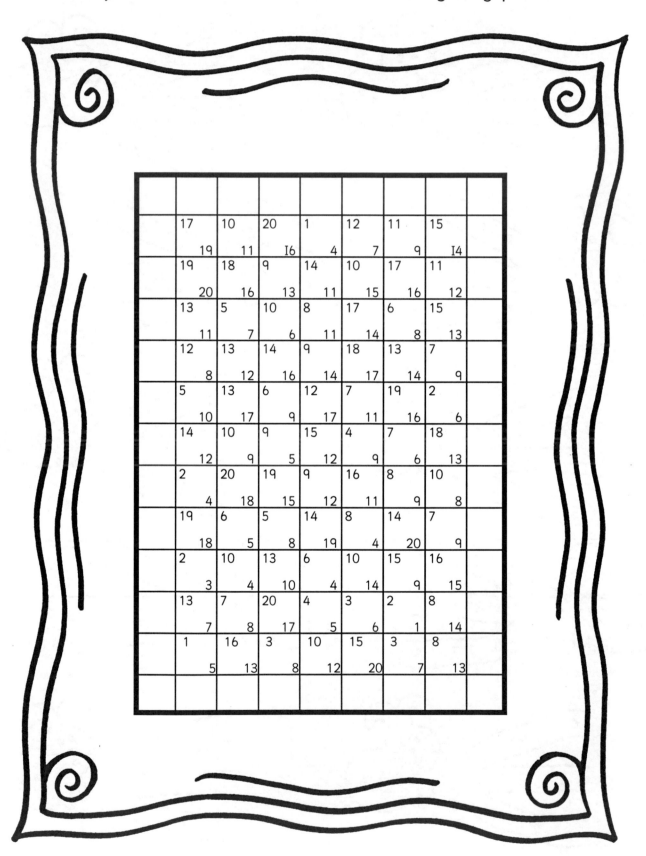

17 19	10 11	20 16	1 4	12 7	11 9	15 14
19 20	18 16	9 13	14 11	10 15	17 16	11 12
13 11	5 7	10 6	8 11	17 14	6 8	15 13
12 8	13 12	14 16	9 14	18 17	13 14	7 9
5 10	13 17	6 9	12 17	7 11	19 16	2 6
14 12	10 9	9 5	15 12	4 9	7 6	18 13
2 4	20 18	19 15	9 12	16 11	8 9	10 8
19 18	6 5	5 8	14 19	8 4	14 20	7 9
2 3	10 4	13 10	6 4	10 14	15 9	16 15
13 7	7 8	20 17	4 5	3 6	2 1	8 14
1 5	16 13	3 8	10 12	15 20	3 7	8 13

Number line time

Cut out the numbers and stick them in the boxes at random.
Use the number line to find the difference between them.

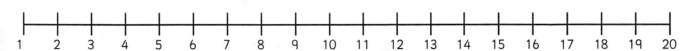

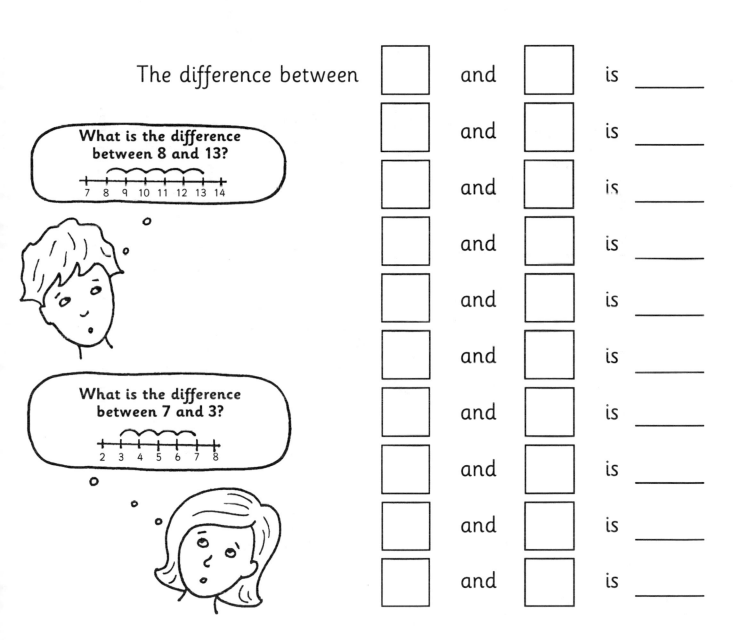

The difference between ☐ and ☐ is _____

and ☐ is _____

and ☐ is _____

and ☐ is _____

and ☐ is _____

and ☐ is _____

and ☐ is _____

and ☐ is _____

and ☐ is _____

and ☐ is _____

What is the difference between 8 and 13?

7 8 9 10 11 12 13 14

What is the difference between 7 and 3?

2 3 4 5 6 7 8

7	15	2	4	20	16	3	9	13	17
10	18	1	19	11	5	12	6	8	14

Hidden toy

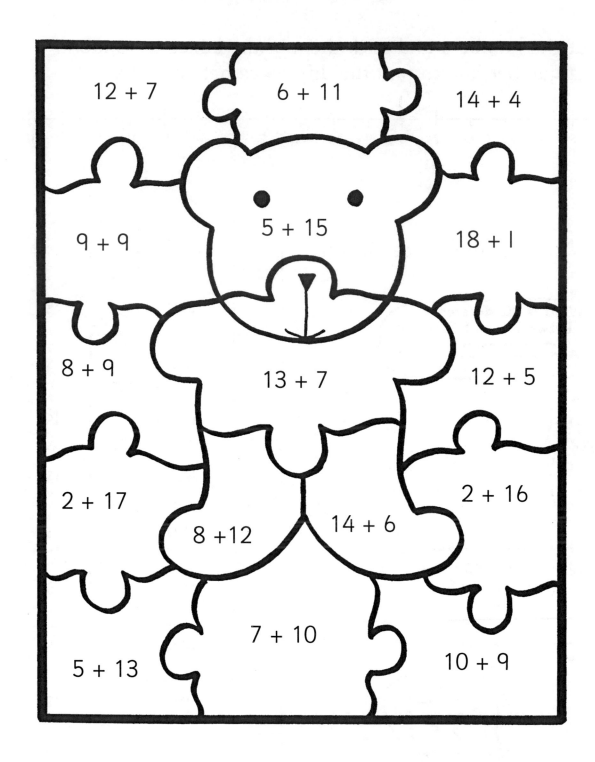

Colour the shapes blue if the total is 17
                   yellow if the total is 18
                   green if the total is 19
                   pink if the total is 20.

Hidden creature

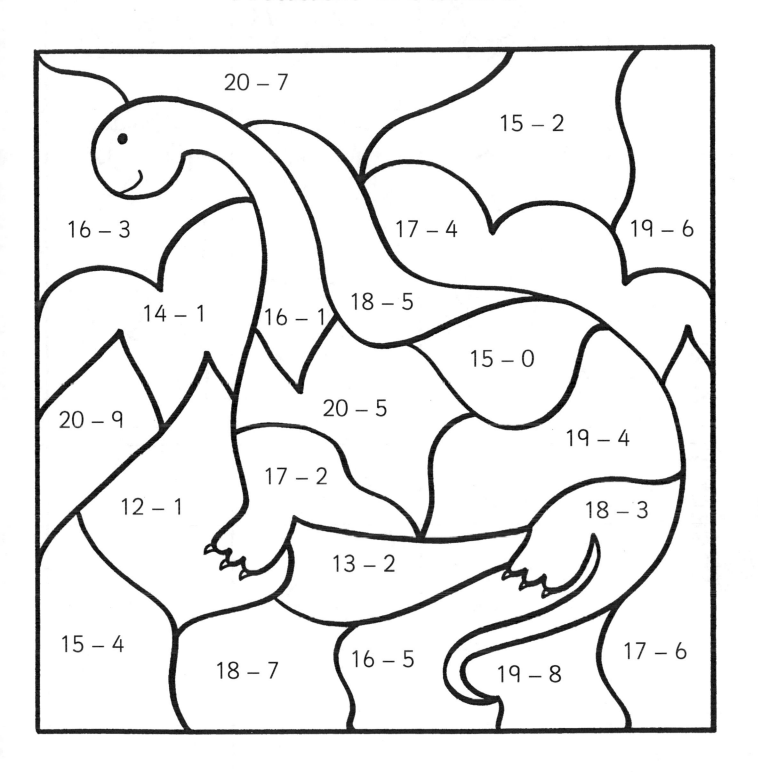

Colour the shapes brown if the difference is 11
blue if the difference is 13
green if the difference is 15.

Insect journey

Starting with the number on each insect, take it on a journey, adding and subtracting as you go. Write the numbers in the flowers.

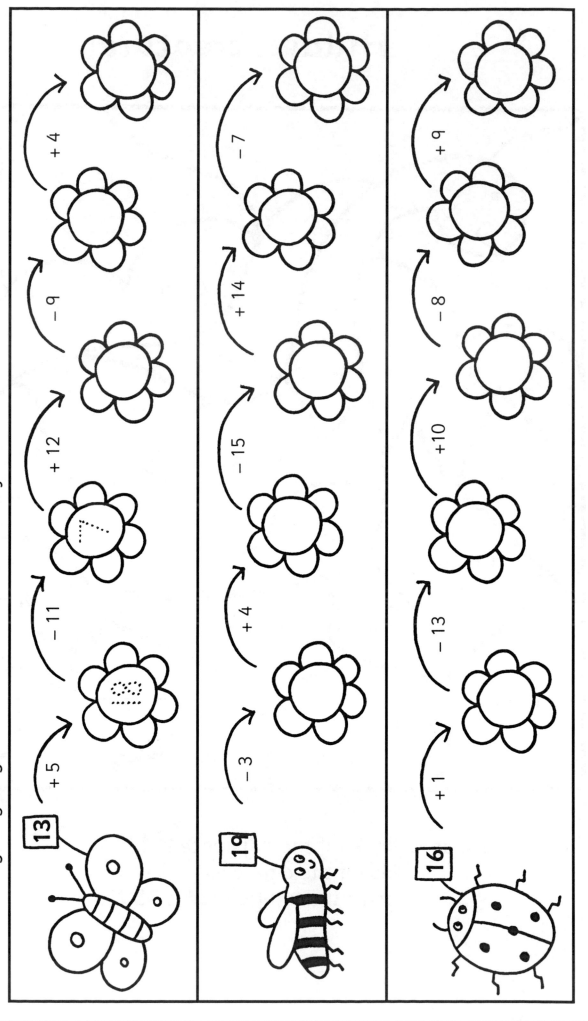

Row 1: 13 → +5 → −11 → +12 → −9 → +4

Row 2: 19 → −3 → +4 → −15 → +14 → −7

Row 3: 16 → +1 → −13 → +10 → −8 → +9

Blow out the candles game

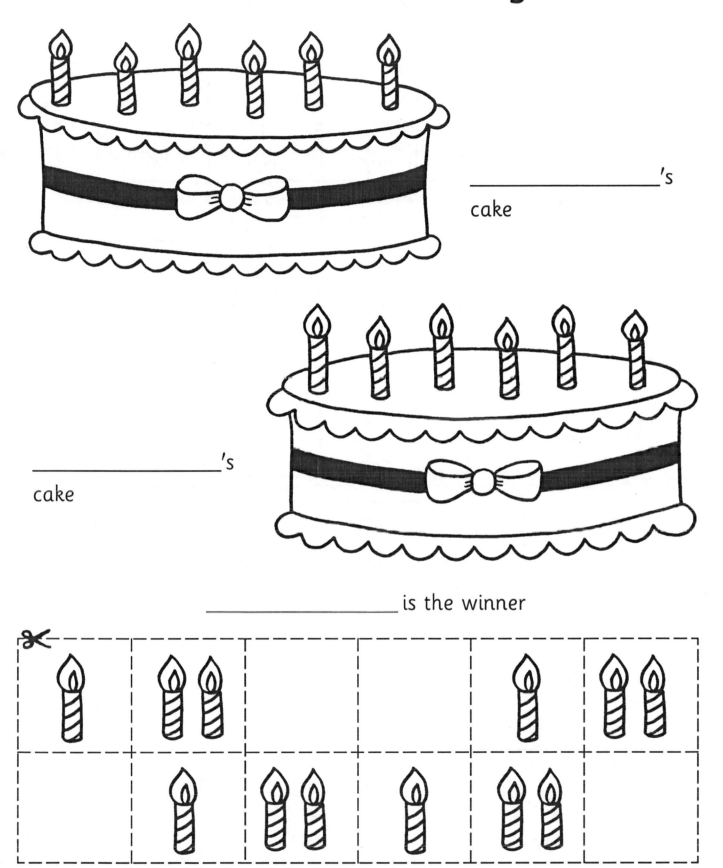

_____'s

cake

_____'s

cake

_____ is the winner

Game for 2 players.
Stick the candles which are at the bottom on to card and cut along the dotted lines. Place the cards face down on a table. The children take it in turns to choose a card. Whatever number of candles is on the card, the same number of candles must be crossed out on that child's cake. If a blank card is chosen, play reverts to the other child. The first child to cross out all the candles is the winner.

Plant the flowers game

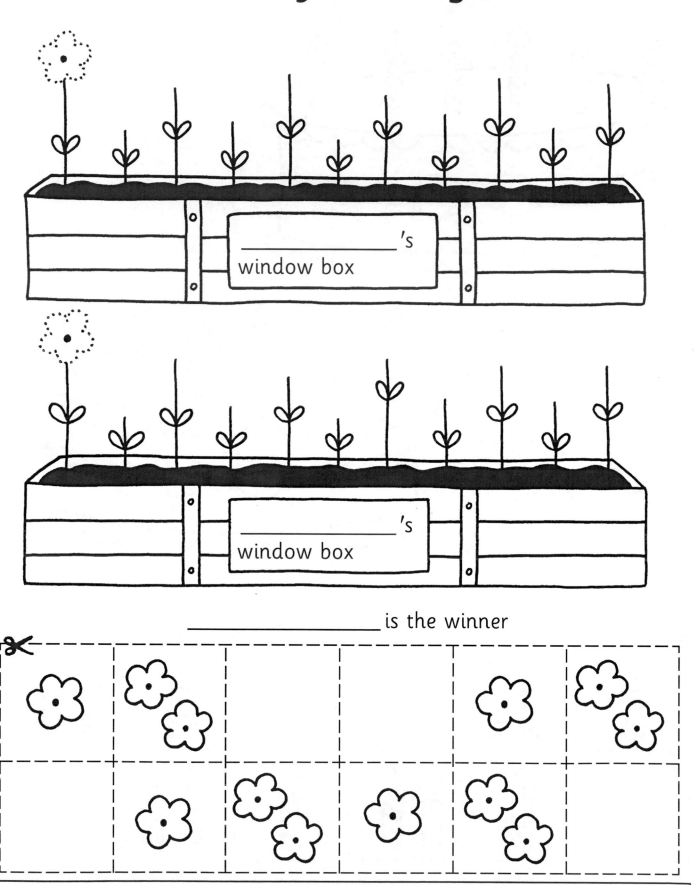

_____'s
window box

_____'s
window box

_____ is the winner

Game for 2 players.
Stick the flowers which are at the bottom on to card and cut along the dotted lines. Place the cards face down on a table. The children take it in turns to choose a card. Whatever number of flowers is on the card, the same number of flowers must be drawn in that child's window box. If a blank card is chosen, play reverts to the other child. The first child to complete all the flowers is the winner.

The teddy bear game

Game for 2 players.
Equipment: 2 dice, 2 crayons (a different colour for each child) and a calculator.
The children take turns to throw the dice. The dice thrower adds the scores together and matches the total to the number on one of the bears. The other child checks the sum on a calculator. If correct, the dice thrower colours in the number on the bear's shirt. If the bear has already been coloured or if the answer is incorrect, then play reverts to the other child. The child with the most bears at the end of the game is the winner.

How to Sparkle at Addition and Subtraction to 20

The smiley face race

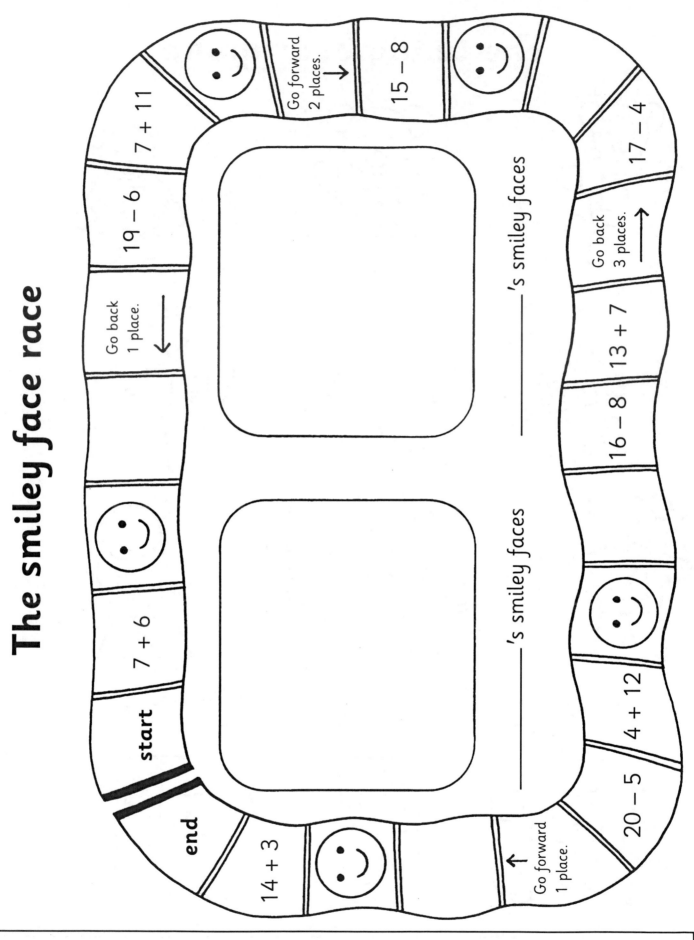

start · 7 + 6 · 7 + 11 · 19 − 6 · Go back 1 place. ↓ · Go forward 2 places. → · 15 − 8 · 17 − 4 · Go back 3 places. ↑ · 13 + 7 · 16 − 8 · 4 + 12 · 20 − 5 · Go forward 1 place. ← · 14 + 3 · end

_____'s smiley faces

_____'s smiley faces

Game for 2 players.
Equipment: a die, 2 counters, a piece of scrap paper and a calculator.
The children take it in turns to throw the die, moving along the track accordingly. If the die thrower lands on a sum, he/she has to write the answer on a piece of paper while the other child checks it on a calculator. If correct, the die thrower draws a smiley face in his or her set. Extra smiley faces can be gained by landing on a smiley face. When both children have reached the end of the track, the winner is the one with the most smiley faces.